The Weather

Bill Bailey

Macdonald/Educational

Managing Editor Chris Milsome
Series Editor Verity Weston
Editor Anne Furniss
Design Peter Benoist
Production Philip Hughes
Picture Research Jackie Newton
                    Lorna Collin

First published 1974
Macdonald and Co. (Publishers) Limited
St. Giles House, 49-50 Poland Street,
London, W1A 2LG

contents

ISBN 0 356 04455 6

Printed by Litografía A. Romero, S. A.
Tenerife (Spain). D. L. 300 - 74

Magic rainmakers

Signs from the gods

Our early ancestors were pathetic, timid creatures. They hunted in gangs to attack one animal. Their idea of hunting was to allow the animal to fall into a pit and then to hit it with stones.

No wonder they were always frightened. They were frightened of the sabre-toothed tiger and the mammoth, they were frightened of each other and, above all, they were frightened of the weather. To them storm clouds were the chariots of the gods, while thunder and lightning were signs of their anger.

Witchdoctors and mistletoe

When man became a farmer he would pray to the gods for sun or rain for his crops. In those days weather was magic and the witchdoctor was the only man who could control it. In many native tribes this belief still holds today.

Even in civilized countries, traces of weather magic still survive. To carry a stinging nettle is supposed to protect a person from lightning, and a house containing black coral or mistletoe will be protected.

The mask of a sun god

▲ This golden mask was found in Peru. The early people of South America worshipped the sun and made masks in its image.

▲ In the Middle Ages everyone was terrified of the weather. These witches are trying to conjure up hail and thunder to frighten someone.

◄ An Australian aborigine "coroboree", or ceremonial dance. The aborigines feel they have a duty to look after all natural things, so they perform a rain-making ceremony.

Is the sun an enemy or a friend?

Pluto   Uranus

Neptune

Saturn: 1,427 million km.
from the sun

Jupiter: 778 million km.
from the sun
Day and night with freezing
temperatures.

A vast ball of flaming gas

Although our sun is just an ordinary
star, it is anything but ordinary to us. It
is a fiery ball of exploding gases
1,306,000 times as big as the earth, and
333,420 times as heavy. The temperature at its centre is about 5,000°C.

Around this incredible furnace rotate
the planets of the solar system, and they
all rely on the sun's rays for their energy.
Planets near the sun absorb huge
amounts, while distant planets receive
very little. If the sun's heat dropped
13% the earth would be covered with
ice, but if it increased by 30% all exist-
ing life forms would be destroyed.

Controlling our way of life

The amount of energy received from the
sun completely controls our life style. In
temperate climates, it is possible to live
and work throughout the year with only
slight changes of clothing.

In countries with hot summers the
whole pattern of life must be changed.
Offices and shops open early and close
at midday to open again in the evening.
Towns and villages are deserted in the
afternoons but a hive of activity in the
cool evenings.

In the opal mines in the Australian
desert, miners work and live under-
ground to escape the heat of the sun.

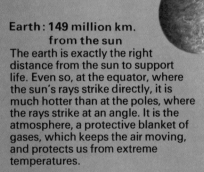

Earth: 149 million km.
from the sun
The earth is exactly the right
distance from the sun to support
life. Even so, at the equator, where
the sun's rays strike directly, it is
much hotter than at the poles, where
the rays strike at an angle. It is the
atmosphere, a protective blanket of
gases, which keeps the air moving,
and protects us from extreme
temperatures.

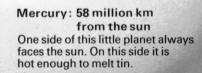

Mercury: 58 million km
from the sun
One side of this little planet always
faces the sun. On this side it is
hot enough to melt tin.

Mars: 228 million km.
from the sun
This planet is warm during the day
but bitterly cold at night.

Venus: 108 million km.
from the sun
This planet is the same size as
earth, but the temperature is 800°C.
(1,472°F.)

The solar system

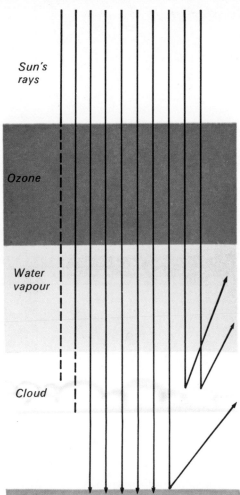

Sun's
rays

Ozone

Water
vapour

Cloud

Earth

▲ Of all the energy received from the sun
only 30-50% is absorbed by the earth. About
30% is reflected back. Some is scattered by
dust particles and water droplets, causing
blue skies and red sunsets, while even more
is absorbed by gases in the air.

▼ The sun can be too strong. In hot
countries, houses are painted white to
reflect heat and walls are thick to keep the
insides cool.

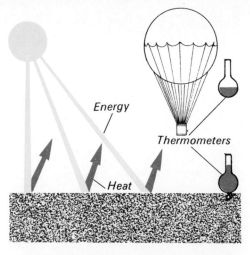

Energy

Thermometers

Heat

▲ The earth absorbs energy and gives it out
in the form of heat. Although the balloon is
closer to the sun, the temperature is colder
than on the ground. Heat comes from the
earth, not from the sun.

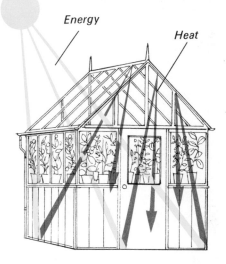

Energy

Heat

▲ Glass is transparent to rays of energy from
the sun, but absorbs and traps heat rays
given off by the earth. The heat is reflected
back, making the greenhouse hotter.

Living with the weather

An unavoidable part of life

No-one can escape from the weather. It controls everything we eat, everything we wear, and often everything we do. A sudden cold spell may make fuel prices soar, while the next week a heat wave could cause a boom in swimwear sales. Sometimes we fight with all our power merely to exist, while at other times it provides us with the pleasures of holidays and the countryside.

A wind that makes men mad

The weather even affects the way we think and act. In the spring and autumn a relentless wind blows south from Central France and sweeps across Provence to the Gulf of Lyons. So unpleasant is this wind that it makes people feel ill and bad-tempered and is even said to have made people go mad.

Bad discipline

Some American scientists have discovered that the weather also affects school-children. They found that pupils were disciplined five times more often in damp weather than they were in dry weather.

It is only recently that scientists have begun to study these aspects of the weather and have come to realize just how large an influence it has on our lives.

▲ A dust storm seen from an aircraft. Wind can whip soil up into the air and turn fields into dry and barren deserts.

▼ Weather has a great influence on industry. In Alaska, men have had to fight for the oil they need. In extreme cold, the equipment may crack and become unuseable.

▲ Freak weather can cause sudden disaster. A severe gust of wind made this huge concrete cooling tower collapse, but left others nearby unharmed.

▲ A man sneezing. Many illnesses are a result of the weather. Bronchitis is known as the English disease because of the number of people who catch it in the damp English winters.

▲ Travel agencies may promise perfect holidays, but even the most expensive cannot guarantee the weather. For people who like the seaside, bad weather can ruin a holiday.

A "discomfort" index

This is a graph drawn up to show the weather conditions people can comfortably work in. People doing light work can work in hotter and more humid weather than those doing manual work. People working in a hot, humid climate which they are not used to can only work comfortably in cooler and drier conditions.

Heavy workers

Light workers

Unacclimatized workers

Temperature — 55°C — 0

Vapour pressure — 30 mm Hg

▼ A patch of hot, humid weather in a crowded city can make people very irritable and bad-tempered. Many bad riots have taken place in this sort of weather.

▲ In spite of complex electronic equipment, few aircraft will take off in fog. The weather has always been a cause of inconvenient delays in all forms of travelling.

At the bottom of a sea of air

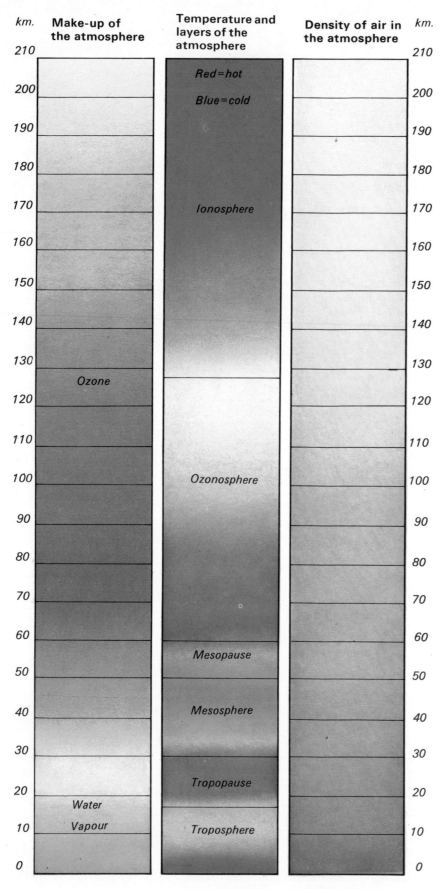

km.	Make-up of the atmosphere	Temperature and layers of the atmosphere	Density of air in the atmosphere	km.
210		Red=hot		210
200		Blue=cold		200
190				190
180				180
170		Ionosphere		170
160				160
150				150
140				140
130				130
120	Ozone			120
110				110
100		Ozonosphere		100
90				90
80				80
70				70
60				60
50		Mesopause		50
40		Mesosphere		40
30				30
20	Water	Tropopause		20
10	Vapour	Troposphere		10
0				0

Vital protection

After the powerful sun, the most important factor in our weather is the atmosphere. This narrow band of gases and water vapour acts like a circular envelope, protecting the earth from vast extremes of heat and cold.

If we had no atmosphere, and particularly no water vapour, life as we know it would not be possible. Without the atmosphere the temperature could rise by day to a blistering 80° C. (176° F.) on the equator. At night, the warmth would escape into outer space so fast that the temperature would drop to −140° C. (−220° F.)

The atmosphere is made up of many layers, all of which play a vital part in our weather and in the existence of life.

Breeding ground of the weather

What must it be like to be a shrimp crawling about at the bottom of a shallow pool? The life we lead is very much the same. Take us out of our sea of air and we would die as quickly as the shrimp when it is brought ashore.

The shallow sea is the troposphere, the lowest layer of the atmosphere. This is the only area in which weather can exist, because of the water vapour it contains. It is this water vapour which causes the towering clouds of a thunderstorm, the gentle snowflake and the vast fury of a hurricane.

Although the air seems boundless to us, in fact it is a very thin layer. If a model of the earth were made to scale, Mount Everest would be hardly noticeable upon its surface. And yet two-thirds of the troposphere, and nearly all our weather, are below the summit of this mountain.

◄ The different layers of the atmosphere blend into one another, but each has its own character. The air's density decreases gradually and temperature varies from layer to layer. But all the water vapour is in the low levels, giving us our weather.

► The heights of various objects in the atmosphere. The picture is not to scale, because most of the action takes place near the ground, whereas the satellite is almost 1,000 km. (620 miles) above Mount Everest. All the weather is level with or below Mount Everest.

Maximum heights of natural and man-made objects in the atmosphere

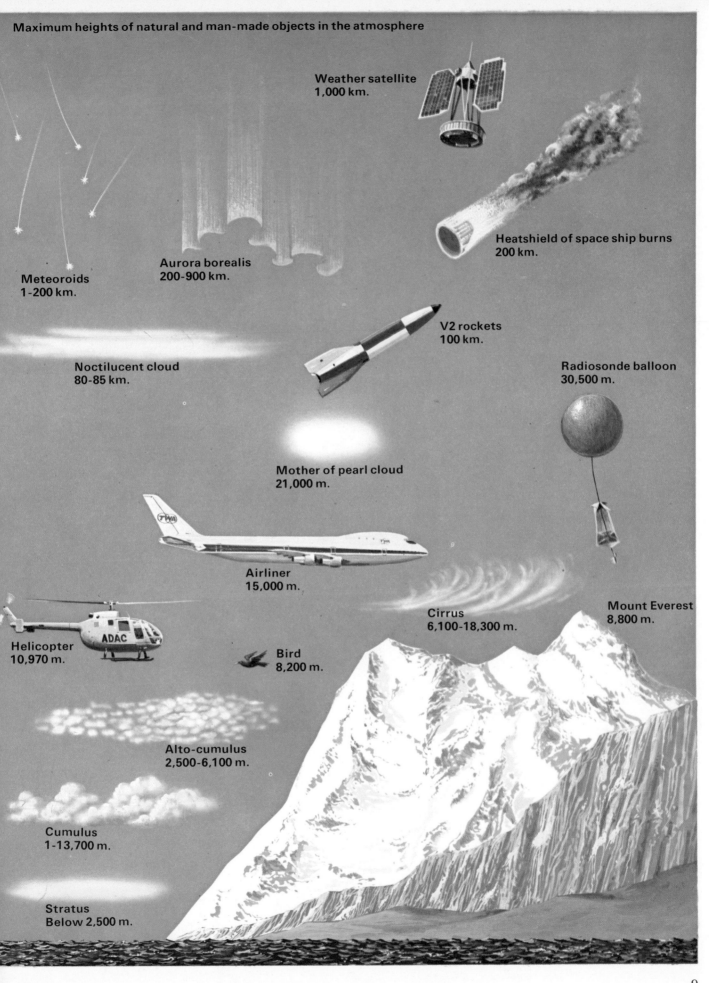

Weather satellite
1,000 km.

Heatshield of space ship burns
200 km.

Aurora borealis
200-900 km.

Meteoroids
1-200 km.

V2 rockets
100 km.

Radiosonde balloon
30,500 m.

Noctilucent cloud
80-85 km.

Mother of pearl cloud
21,000 m.

Airliner
15,000 m.

Mount Everest
8,800 m.

Cirrus
6,100-18,300 m.

Helicopter
10,970 m.

Bird
8,200 m.

Alto-cumulus
2,500-6,100 m.

Cumulus
1-13,700 m.

Stratus
Below 2,500 m.

Air pressure the invisible burden

A simple mercury barometer

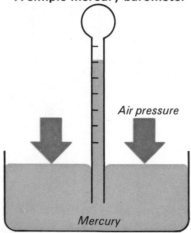

▲ An instrument for measuring air pressure is called a barometer. The pressure of air pushing on the bowl keeps the liquid up the tube. To make your own, see Page 44.

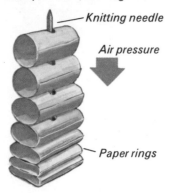

▲ This pile of paper rings shows why pressure varies with height. As more rings are added to the pile, the weight on the bottom one becomes greater, and it is squashed. Pressure in the atmosphere is the same. It is greatest at sea level and decreases with height.

A most important discovery

In 1644, an Italian scientist named Torricelli discovered that air has weight. He turned a tube full of mercury upside down and put it in a bowl of mercury. The mercury did not run down the tube into the bowl. This was because the air above the bowl was pushing down on it, so the level of mercury in the bowl could not rise.

People now realized that air must push down on everything. On each human being there is a constant pressure of air. But pressure also depends on height. The pressure is greatest at sea level, so the higher you go, the less pressure there is.

It is this air pressure which governs our weather and, if we know the pressure, enables us to understand it.

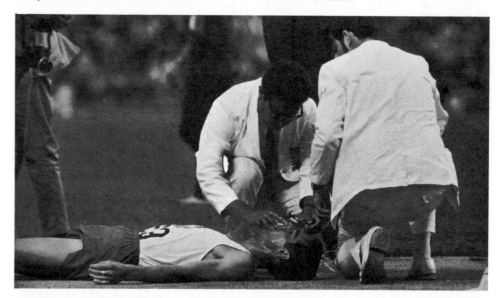

▲ An athlete passes out from lack of oxygen. A person's body is used to the air pressure at the height at which he lives. If he moves to a higher place, he will find it difficult to breathe.

◄ The weight of air pressing down on a person at sea level is enormous; it is equal to the weight of a small car. We do not notice it because within our bodies is an equal force pressing outwards.

▶ A map showing pressure curves. Isobars, lines of equal pressure, surround areas of high or low pressure. Air pressure is measured in millibars and marked on the isobars. On average, pressure at sea level is 1,000 mbs.

The changing face of the weather

Air pressure changes constantly, from place to place and from hour to hour. Because of these changes, every weather station keeps a close watch on air pressure.

A weather forecaster receives the air pressure from a large number of stations and plots them on a map. He then draws a line through all the stations with the same pressure. These lines are called isobars and look very like contour lines on a map.

A map drawn with isobars looks like a series of small ponds with ripples. At the centre of each rippled pond will be an area of low or high pressure. Each pattern has its own weather, so a glance at the isobars will give a good idea of the overall weather.

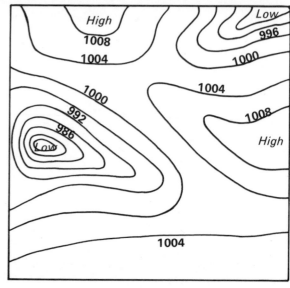

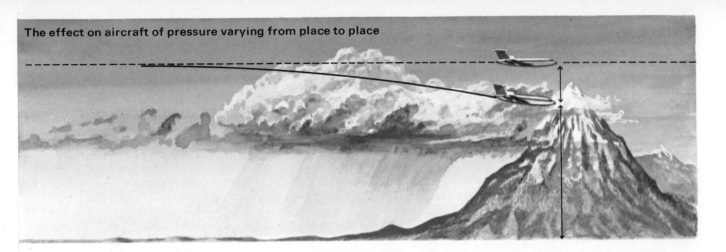

The effect on aircraft of pressure varying from place to place

▲ Pressure varies from place to place. An aircraft sets its altimeter (an aneroid barometer) at the correct pressure for the place it is leaving.

▲ On its journey, the aircraft may pass through an area of lower pressure. The altimeter will then read the wrong height, and the pilot must reset it.

▲ If it is not reset, the height given by the altimeter will not be the height at which the aircraft is flying. In bad visibility, this could cause a crash.

An altimeter

▼ Because pressure varies with height, aircraft can use barometers to measure how high they are. One millibar represents 9 m. (30 ft.). An altimeter is an aneroid barometer, in which a vacuum measures the changes in pressure, not a level of liquid. A project on Page 45 shows how to make an aneroid barometer.

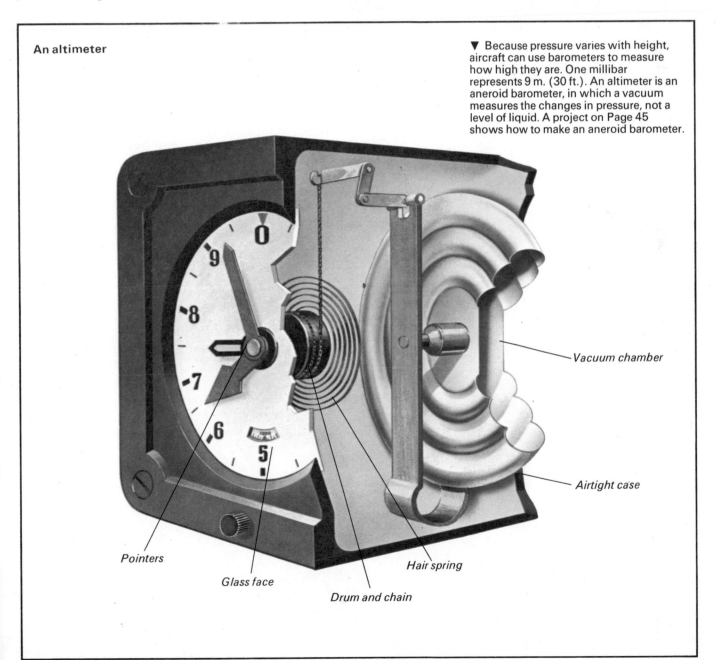

Vacuum chamber

Airtight case

Pointers

Glass face

Drum and chain

Hair spring

Exploring the air about us

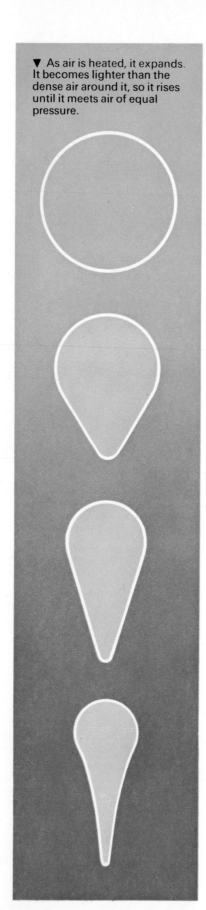

▼ As air is heated, it expands. It becomes lighter than the dense air around it, so it rises until it meets air of equal pressure.

▲ In 1785, the first hot air balloon crossed the English Channel, carrying scientific instruments. It was so heavy that the balloonists had to strip to keep it in the air.

▲ A radiosonde balloon is launched. It will carry weather-recording instruments into the atmosphere. To make it rise, it is filled with hydrogen, a gas which is lighter than air.

Up, up in the air

In the 19th century, the sport of ballooning was very popular. News of a balloon ascent would draw huge crowds. People had clothes with balloons on them, sang songs about balloons and were altogether balloon-mad. And all this excitement was due to the fact that hot air rises.

Jacques Charles, a French chemist, discovered that if air is heated it expands. Expanding air becomes lighter than the air around it and so rises. This creates an area of low pressure. In the same way cold air is heavy and sinks and creates a high pressure area.

A constant cycle

Air around the earth behaves in the same way. Near the equator, it becomes very hot, expands and rises. This creates an area of low pressure and the surrounding air rushes in to fill the gap. At the poles, cold heavy air sinks. It pushes downwards and outwards and creates an area of high pressure.

Rising air cools, so hot, rising air at the equator cools and sinks down between the equator and the poles. This creates another area of high pressure, with low pressure areas on either side.

Air moving between these different pressure areas forms the wind system of the world. The effect of the spin of the earth and land masses make this a very complicated system indeed.

▼ As air heats, it rises. Over open country and towns, air heats rapidly. Currents of air called thermals begin to rise. Birds can gain height effortlessly by circling around thermals and being carried up on the hot air.

▼ Thick woodland heats very slowly, so there are rarely any thermals.

Path of bird

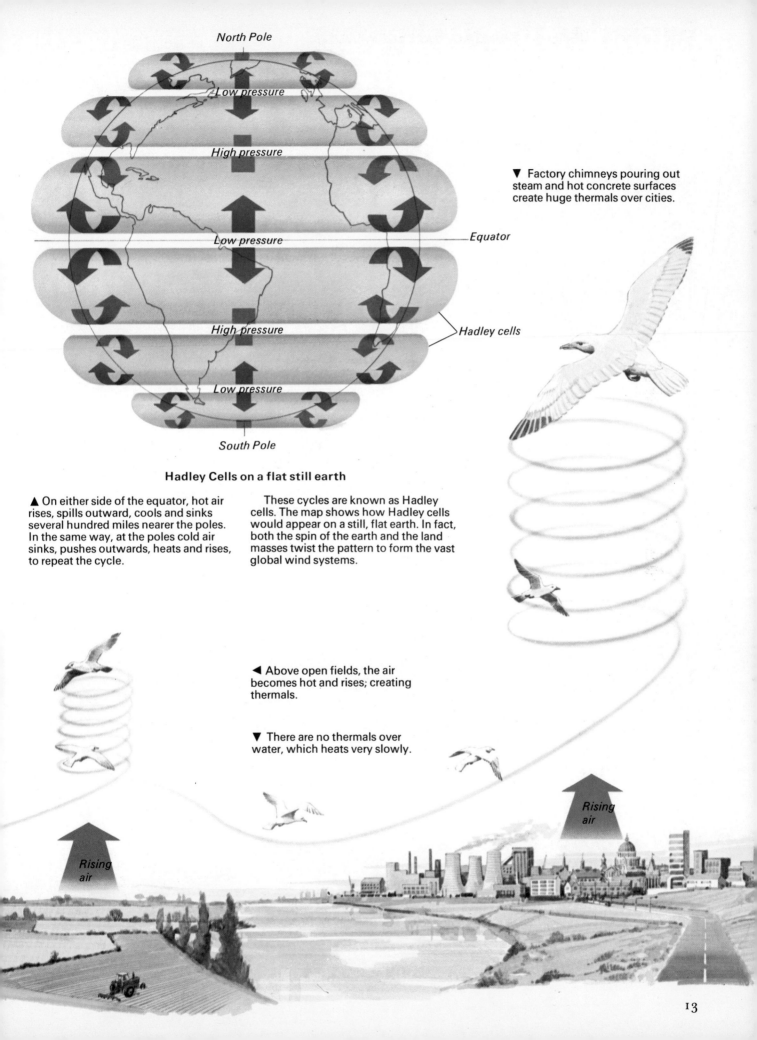

North Pole

Low pressure

High pressure

Low pressure —————————————— *Equator*

High pressure

Low pressure

South Pole

▼ Factory chimneys pouring out steam and hot concrete surfaces create huge thermals over cities.

Hadley cells

Hadley Cells on a flat still earth

▲ On either side of the equator, hot air rises, spills outward, cools and sinks several hundred miles nearer the poles. In the same way, at the poles cold air sinks, pushes outwards, heats and rises, to repeat the cycle.

These cycles are known as Hadley cells. The map shows how Hadley cells would appear on a still, flat earth. In fact, both the spin of the earth and the land masses twist the pattern to form the vast global wind systems.

◄ Above open fields, the air becomes hot and rises; creating thermals.

▼ There are no thermals over water, which heats very slowly.

Rising air

Rising air

Winds and waves the weather and the sea

► The "trade" winds, named after the ancient word for track or path, can be seen to their best advantage in the Southern Hemisphere. In the North, the great land masses tend to create other systems.

Winds of the world

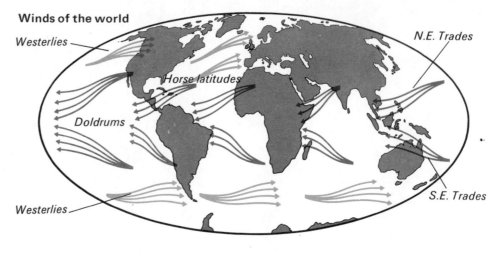

Westerlies — N.E. Trades — *Horse latitudes* — *Doldrums* — *Westerlies* — S.E. Trades

Measuring the wind

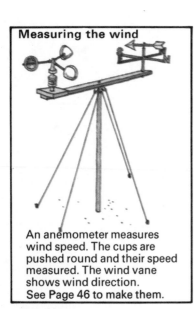

An anemometer measures wind speed. The cups are pushed round and their speed measured. The wind vane shows wind direction. See Page 46 to make them.

The Beaufort wind scale

▼ In 1806, Sir Francis Beaufort, a British admiral, worked out a scale for measuring the speed of the wind at sea. This shows how it can be used on land.

Free coal

Until the introduction of steam in the 19th century, men relied upon the winds to guide their ships around the world. This meant that the trade and prosperity of many people and even of whole nations depended on the weather.

Because of this, the winds were one of the earliest weather systems to be studied. Many areas have strange names dating back to the days of the old sailing ships.

The Horse Latitudes, an area of light, variable winds, is named after the ships which went to the New World. If one of these ships was becalmed in this area, the horses on board would have to be killed and thrown overboard to save drinking water.

Storms and giant waves

The wind systems of the world can give steady winds which blow ships safely and quickly from port to port. But these same systems can make the sea a place of terror for the sailor.

In an area called the Roaring Forties, strong south-westerly winds travelling across thousands of miles of open sea can whip up the surface into huge waves which can wreck ships.

A storm at sea may cause large waves many hundreds of miles away. Some of the worst hurricane damage has been caused by giant waves which sweep inland and flood the countryside. In Pakistan in 1970, nearly one million people died as a result of a giant wave caused by a storm.

▼ **Force 1** (2-5 k.p.h.)
Smoke drifts but wind vanes do not move.

▼ **Force 2** (6-11 k.p.h.)
Light breeze. Leaves rustle and wind vanes move.

▼ **Force 3** (12-19 k.p.h.)
Gentle breeze. Leaves and small twigs move.

▼ **Force 4** (20-29 k.p.h.)
Moderate breeze. Small branches move. Dust raised.

▼ **Force 5** (30-39 k.p.h.)
Fresh breeze. Small leaved trees sway.

▼ **Force 6** (40-50 k.p.h.)
Strong breeze. Large branches move. Telephone wires whistle.

Sailing ships reached perfection in the days of the tea-clippers. Tea is a cargo which spoils easily and so must be transported fast. The clippers used to race each other, and the record was 702 km. (436 miles) in one day.

▼ **Force 7** (51-61 k.p.h.) Moderate gale. Whole trees sway.

▼ **Force 8** (62-74 k.p.h.) Fresh gale. Walking difficult; twigs break off trees.

▼ **Force 9** (75-87 k.p.h.) Strong gale. Chimney pots brought down.

▼ **Force 10** (88-102 k.p.h.) Whole gale. Considerable damage. Trees uprooted.

▼ **Force 11** (103-120 k.p.h.) Storm. Widespread damage.

▼ **Force 12** (Over 120 k.p.h.) Hurricane. Whole area laid waste.

The monsoon a way of life

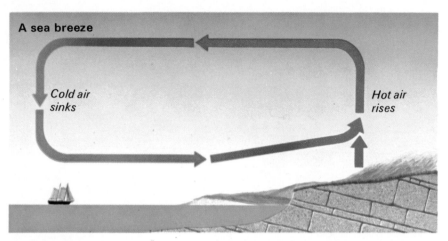

A sea breeze

Cold air sinks

Hot air rises

Summer and winter winds

If the world was all land or all sea, winds would appear as steady systems like the Roaring Forties or the Trade Winds. But the earth is made up of large masses of land and great areas of sea, so the systems are very complicated.

The main reason for this is that land absorbs heat far more quickly than the sea. It also cools down more quickly. As air above a land mass heats up it rises, causing an area of low pressure. Cooler air from surrounding high pressure areas rushes in to take its place.

When winter comes and the land mass becomes very cold, the reverse happens. Land cools far quicker than the sea, so the heavy, cold air sinks and is squeezed outwards from the cold land. This gives a complete reversal of wind direction between winter and summer.

▲ Land heats up faster than the sea. During the day the air over land becomes hot and rises, and cold air moves in from the sea to take its place. At night, the land cools down more quickly than the sea and the reverse happens.

▼ Continents also get hotter than oceans, so the same process takes place. During the summer, hot air rises from the continents, creating a low pressure area, and winds blow in from the sea to the land. In winter, the winds blow from the land to the sea. These winds are the monsoons.

▼ An Indian farmer and his wife watch with relief as the monsoon "breaks". Their lives and those of millions of others depend on these rains, as their main food is rice. Without the rains, the crop would fail, and there would be widespread starvation.

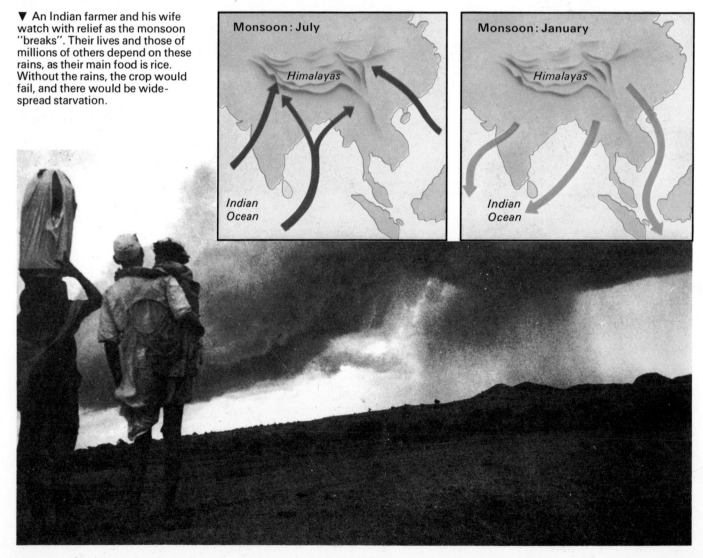

Monsoon: July

Himalayas

Indian Ocean

Monsoon: January

Himalayas

Indian Ocean

Areas of the world affected by the monsoon

A giant land and sea breeze

An example of this system of winds is the Indian monsoon. Pressure over Asia becomes low during the Northern Hemisphere's summer, while it is high over the Indian Ocean. This causes winds known as the South West Monsoon.

As they blow over vast areas of sea, these winds collect moisture, which they deposit as rain over the parched lands. Chiripunji, on the slopes of the Himalayas, receives the full force of this monsoon. It has over 10,160 mm. (400 ins.) of rain a year.

As the sun returns to the Southern Hemisphere, a high pressure area builds up over Asia. The winds change direction, blowing cold from the dry land, and India has its dry season.

Life or death to the people

For the Indian peasant, the most important event of the year is the day when the rain-bearing monsoon clouds roll in from the Arabian Sea.

The whole life style of the people of India is based on the monsoon. Even a delay of a few weeks in the coming of the monsoon can cause widespread droughts and famine.

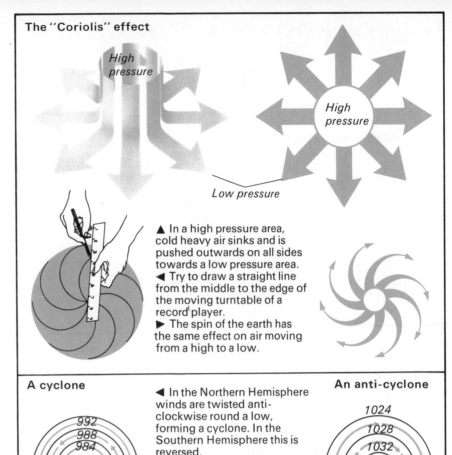

The "Coriolis" effect

High pressure

High pressure

Low pressure

▲ In a high pressure area, cold heavy air sinks and is pushed outwards on all sides towards a low pressure area.
◄ Try to draw a straight line from the middle to the edge of the moving turntable of a record player.
► The spin of the earth has the same effect on air moving from a high to a low.

A cyclone

992
988
984
Low

◄ In the Northern Hemisphere winds are twisted anti-clockwise round a low, forming a cyclone. In the Southern Hemisphere this is reversed.

► In the Northern Hemisphere winds are twisted clockwise round a high, or anticyclone. In the Southern Hemisphere this is reversed.

An anti-cyclone

1024
1028
1032
High

◄ This Malayan house is built on stilts. It is dry now, but when the monsoon breaks it will be up to floor level in water.

▲ Rice growing in paddy fields. Rice is an ideal crop for monsoon regions as it requires hot sun followed by heavy rain.

Clouds and their formation

How clouds form

Air can only hold a certain amount of water vapour. If there is too much water vapour it "condenses" to form a cloud, a mass of tiny water droplets.
Hot air can hold a large amount of water vapour, but cold air can only hold a little. When hot air rises, it cools, so it can no longer hold the same amount of water.

◀ The kettle is pouring more water vapour into the air than it can hold. The excess condenses to form steam, or cloud.

▶ Warm air is cooled by the cold air from the fridge. It can no longer hold its water vapour, so cloud forms.

▲ An island bakes in the sun and hot air rises. The rising air cools and cannot hold its water vapour, so a small cloud forms.

▲ Air blowing towards a mountain is forced to rise up the sides. It cools and releases its water vapour as a cloud near the summit.

▲ Warm and cold air do not mix. Warm air rides up the invisible side of a mass of cold air and cools. Wispy clouds begin to form.

Alto-stratus (As)
2,500-6,100 m.

Alto-cumulus (Ac)
2,500-6,100 m.

Stratus (St)
Below 2,500 m.

Strato-cumulus (Sc)
Below 2,500 m.

Nimbo-stratus (Ns)
Below 2,500 m.

Cirrus (Ci)
6,100-18,300 m.

Cumulo-nimbus (Cb)
1-18,300 m.

Cumulus (Cu)
1-13,700 m.

Rain a mixed blessing

The growth of a raindrop

The water droplets in clouds are far too small to fall as rain. Raindrops form when there are solid particles in a cloud. These may be ice, tiny pieces of salt evaporated with water from the sea, or specks of carbon from the smoke of fires and factory chimneys.

Each particle attracts little water droplets, which cluster round and combine, forming a drop. The drops then run into each other and grow bigger. When they get too heavy for the cloud to support, they fall as rain.

The type of rain which falls depends on the size of particle around which the drops form. Big drops from thunderclouds may be 25 times the size of drops which fall as drizzle.

Man-made rain

For centuries, people have tried to make rain. Witchdoctors have performed elaborate ceremonies to persuade the gods to drop rain. In the 19th century in France they exploded fireworks in clouds, and as recently as 1970 an aborigine rainmaking ceremony took place during a drought in Australia.

Most modern rain-making is more scientific. People try to charge the cloud with the necessary particles. These are either dropped by an aircraft from above, or they are injected into the base by means of smoke. Some of these methods have been successful, but it will be a long time before we can control the weather to our liking.

▲ Rice growing in flooded paddy fields. Millions of people depend on rice for their food, so to them the amount of rain which falls is vital.

▲ Too much rain can be disastrous, and many people lose their lives in floods every year. This artificial hill has been built for the protection of people and animals when there is a flood.

▶ Too little rain can also cause disasters. No plants will grow in this soil, which has baked hard and cracked from lack of rain.

▲ "Rain stopped play" is a common end to sporting events in mild climates. In countries which do not suffer from a lack of water, rain is often looked on as a nuisance.

▼ Yet rain can transform an apparently dead landscape into a place of beauty. During the few days when rain does fall, the desert springs into glorious life.

World rainfall

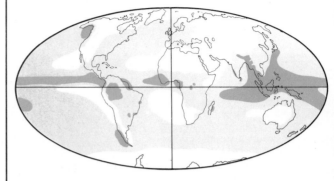

▲ The map shows the average world annual rainfall, which is about 1,016 mm. (40 ins.). The dark patches show the areas of heaviest rainfall. Only a quarter of the rain falls on land.

The water cycle

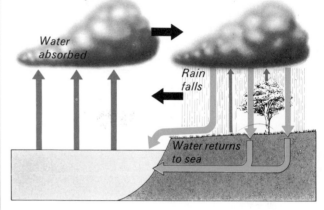

Water absorbed

Rain falls

Water returns to sea

▲ Rain is not new water, but water which has evaporated. Rain falls and forms rivers and lakes which run into the sea. Water from all these evaporates, forms clouds and falls as rain again.

A rain gauge

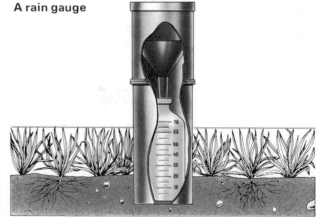

▲ Rain is measured by a rain gauge, a tin containing a funnel in a marked jar. The gauge must be placed above grass level so that no water can splash into it. To make your own rain gauge, see Page 45.

Air masses weather on the move

Sources of air masses

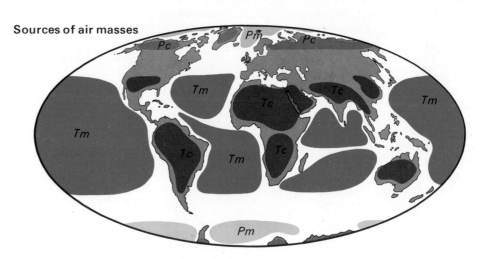

▶ The regions where air masses form are vast areas of land or sea with similar conditions. Continental (c) air masses are dry and maritime (m) air masses are wet. So an air mass forming over the Sahara Desert would be a tropical continental (Tc) air mass and would be hot and dry. An air mass which formed over the Arctic Ocean would be a polar maritime (Pm) air mass and would be cold and wet.

Air masses on the move

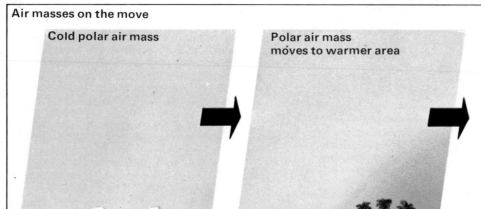

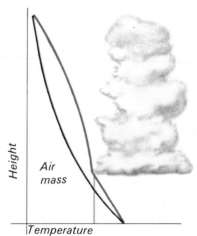

Cold polar air mass

Polar air mass moves to warmer area

▲ A polar air mass usually forms over cold oceans or continents near the Arctic Circle or Antarctica. It is cold and can be either wet or dry.

▲ As the polar air mass moves towards the equator, air in contact with the ground becomes warmer. The main bulk of the air remains cold.

▲ The red line shows air rising into the cold air mass. The mass is warm at the bottom but cold higher up, so the air can rise to great heights, forming tall clouds.

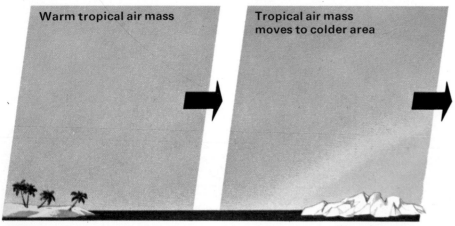

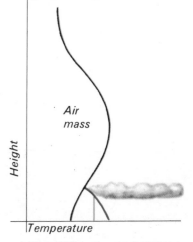

Warm tropical air mass

Tropical air mass moves to colder area

▲ A tropical air mass forms over sub-tropical oceans or low-latitude deserts. It can be either wet or dry, but will always be warm.

▲ When the tropical air mass begins to move over colder ground, the base gradually cools down. The rest of the air mass remains warm.

▲ The red line shows air rising into a warm air mass, which has cooled at the bottom but is still warm higher up. The rising air stops when it meets the warmer air.

Changeable weather

In many temperate countries, it is possible to have warm, moist weather conditions one day and bitterly cold, dry conditions the next day. This is not because of the amount of sunshine or because the air has become colder. It means that the air has completely changed. The warm, moist air has been pushed right away by new air which is cold and dry.

Throughout the world, this struggle between great masses of cold and warm air is taking place. An air mass forms when air is stationary for a long period of time over a vast area of land or sea with similar conditions. Air which rests over a hot, dry desert will become hot and dry, while air resting over the frozen Arctic Ocean will become cold and wet.

▲ These conditions are called unstable, and the tall clouds which form are normally great thunder-clouds like this one, with an anvil-shaped top made of ice.

▲ These conditions are called stable. The air cannot rise, so low, flat clouds form and smoke, fog and drizzle are trapped underneath. This is called an inversion.

Giants of weather

As an air mass begins to move, it brings changes in weather to the areas over which it passes. A cold air mass usually brings good visibility and dry, clear air. A warm air mass, on the other hand, may bring muggy weather with fog and drizzle.

Moving air masses also change themselves. A cold air mass moving across warmer land or sea begins to warm up at the bottom, and a warm air mass going over colder ground will cool down at the bottom.

The main body of an air mass brings fairly settled conditions; it is at the edges that the great changes occur. Cold and warm air will not mix, so the edges, or fronts, between cold and warm air masses are the scenes of battles between the weather giants.

▼ Running along the edges of fronts between air masses are strong winds called jet streams. These are narrow belts of high speed wind, with light winds on each side, which occur high in the troposphere. Their speeds can reach 483 k.p.h. (300 m.p.h.). They are caused by temperature differences between two air masses.

▼ A jet stream can make a great difference to the speed of an aircraft. If an aircraft travelling from the U.S. to Europe (*A*) has a jet stream following it, this can take hours off its flight time.

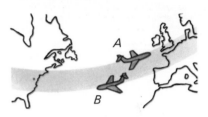

▲ If an aircraft going from Europe to the U.S. (*B*) runs into a jet stream it may take much longer to reach its destination.

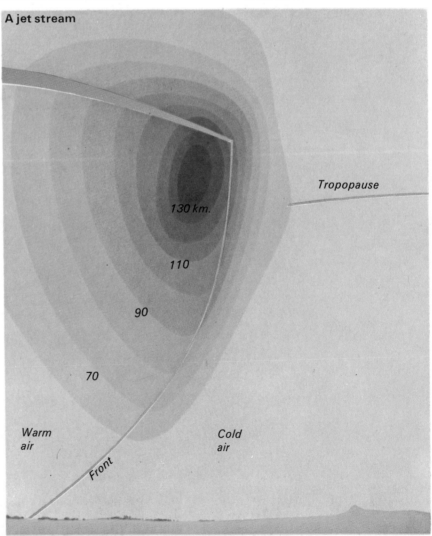

A jet stream

Tropopause

130 km.

110

90

70

Warm air

Cold air

Front

Giants at war fronts and depressions

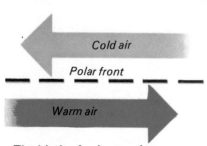

The birth of a depression

▲ In the Northern Hemisphere, polar air is separated from tropical air by the polar front. This lies from east to west and the air flows in opposite directions on either side of it.

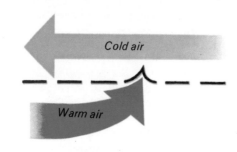

▲ Sometimes, a disturbance causes a bump to appear in the front. Warm air begins to edge into the cold air and sets up a wave that becomes bigger as it travels eastward along the polar front.

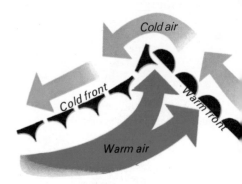

▲ A low pressure area forms at the crest of the wave and winds begin to blow round it. The two sides begin to close up, forming a warm and a cold front. This is now called a depression.

Cross-section of a mature depression

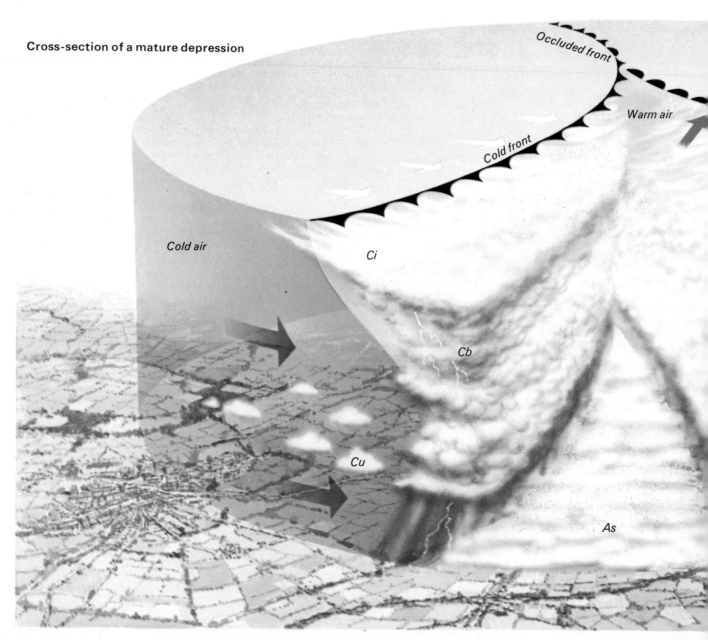

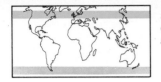

A topic of conversation

Visitors to England often say that all the English can talk about is the weather. It is certainly true that the English can never be sure what their weather will do next. A few days of perfect sunny weather may be followed by a week of cold drizzle.

This is because the British Isles are near a line called the polar front, where the great polar air masses meet air masses from the tropics. The changeable weather is due to tremendous battles being fought between the rival air masses.

Warm and cold fronts

Cold air masses and warm air masses never mix. The one which is moving faster will push the other one out of its way, and the line where they meet is called a front.

If a warm air mass is moving faster it will run up the side of the cold air mass and push it away; this is a warm front. Clouds get gradually lower and it rains for a few hours.

If the cold air mass travels faster, this burrows under the warm air mass and forms a cold front. This often results in thunderstorms and showers.

How a depression dies

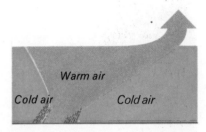

1. An occlusion

▲ As the cold front overtakes the warm front, the middle section of warm air is lifted up above the earth's surface. When this happens the depression begins to "fill" and disappear. This lifted front is called an occlusion.

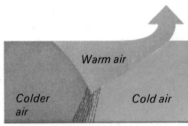

2. A cold occlusion

▲ When the cold front overtakes the warm front the warm section is lifted above the earth's surface. If this cold air is colder than the air in front, a cold occlusion is formed.

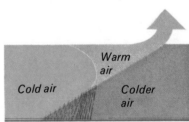

3. A warm occlusion

▲ If the air behind the cold front has warmed up a little, it will rise up the warm front and create a warm occlusion. This often surprises people as there is a sudden increase in the violence of the rain.

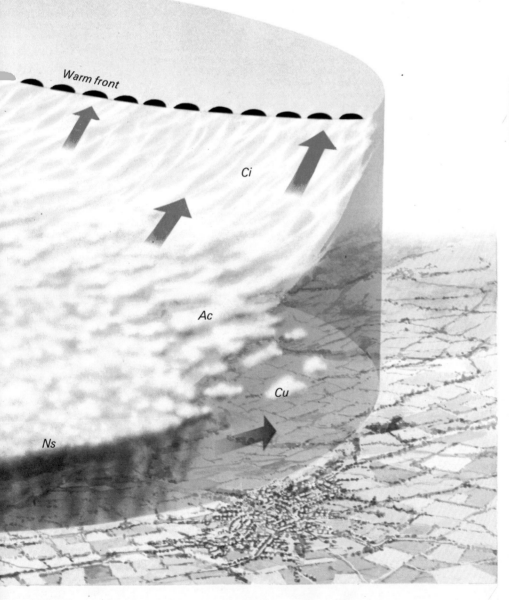

25

Storm!

▲ Benjamin Franklin flew a kite with a metal key on it to prove that there is electricity in storms. This was very dangerous as electricity is attracted to metal.

▶ The huge, pointed Empire State Building in New York has been struck by lightning as often as 48 times in one day.

▼ A tornado is the most violent of storms. It is really a tiny depression. The winds spin round very fast and create a funnel. This sucks things up like a gigantic vacuum cleaner.

▲ This old French gentleman is being ultra cautious. He fears he may be struck by lightning while using his umbrella. The high point will act as a conductor, while the trailing wire is supposed to carry the lightning harmlessly to earth. In fact it would not work.

The power of an atomic bomb

Every day, there are 45,000 thunderstorms somewhere on earth, and each storm may easily be as powerful as a hydrogen bomb. In 1800, crabs fell from the sky during a storm in Worcester, England, which is over 64 km. (40 miles) from the sea. The tremendous updraughts of air in a thundercloud had scooped up water from the sea and taken the crabs with it.

Thunderstorms often occur when visibility is good and the air unstable. First, little fluffy cumulus clouds appear. They grow bigger and bigger until the tops are high enough for ice to form. The top becomes a wispy, icy cloud which spreads out into an anvil shape. Once formed, a thundercloud has the energy to survive for many hours.

Electrical fireworks

Thunder and lightning are spectacular effects of a storm. Lightning looks forked or jagged because it is an electric current trying to find the quickest path to the earth. Thunder is the noise produced by the sudden expansion of air heated by lightning.

The charge in a thunderstorm is produced by the continual splitting of falling rain drops. As they split, the positively charged parts are carried high up into the cloud, while the negatively charged parts remain at the bottom.

This sets up positive charges on the ground below, and suddenly the bolt strikes. The current flashes between the top and bottom of the cloud and from the bottom to the ground, striking the tallest projecting object.

▲ A hail stone cut in half. Hail forms when a water drop is carried above the freezing level in an upward gust. It freezes and, as it falls, collides with other drops which give it a coating of clear ice. This may happen many times before it falls to earth. Each layer of ice means another trip to the top of the cloud.

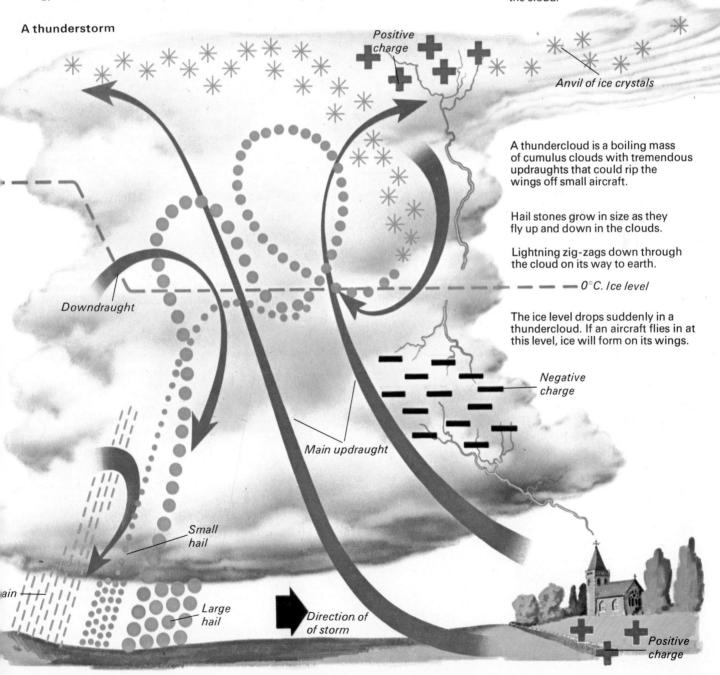

A thunderstorm

Positive charge

Anvil of ice crystals

A thundercloud is a boiling mass of cumulus clouds with tremendous updraughts that could rip the wings off small aircraft.

Hail stones grow in size as they fly up and down in the clouds.

Lightning zig-zags down through the cloud on its way to earth.

— — 0°C. Ice level

The ice level drops suddenly in a thundercloud. If an aircraft flies in at this level, ice will form on its wings.

Negative charge

Downdraught

Main updraught

Small hail

Rain

Large hail

Direction of of storm

Positive charge

27

The furious hurricane

Pillars of cloud

Main updraught

160 km.	113 km.	80 km.	48 km.	
Pressure falling	Pressure 998 mb.	Pressure 982 mb.	Pressure 967 mb.	Pressure 945 mb.
Wind N.N.E.	Wind N.	Wind N.W.	Wind W.N.W.	No wind
Force 6	Force 9	Force 12	Force 12	Clear sky, warm

▲ This satellite picture of a hurricane shows clearly the swirling bands of cloud which surround the clear eye in the centre.

The most terrible storms of all

The most destructive type of storm is the tropical hurricane. These happen in many parts of the world, and are given many different names. In Australia they are called willy-willies and in Asia cyclones or typhoons. Yet wherever they occur they are feared more than any other type of weather.

It has been estimated that a tropical storm generates as much energy in one second as ten atomic bombs. Since 1900, hurricanes have destroyed over £5,000 million of property in the U.S. alone. This damage is caused by winds which are strong enough to blow down houses and vast waves which destroy harbours and shipping.

A depression with a difference

A hurricane is a depression, but the difference is that warm surface air rises rapidly to great heights, forming pillars of cloud. As it does so, the water vapour condenses to form thousands of tons of heavy rain. The rain is accompanied by tremendous winds which can reach speeds of 322 k.p.h. (200 m.p.h.).

In the middle of the storm, there is a perfectly clear patch. This is the "eye", an outstanding feature of tropical storms. It is a circular area, maybe 48 km. (30 miles) across with clear blue skies and no wind.

After the eye has passed, the howling winds and rain return, but now the wind blows in exactly the opposite direction.

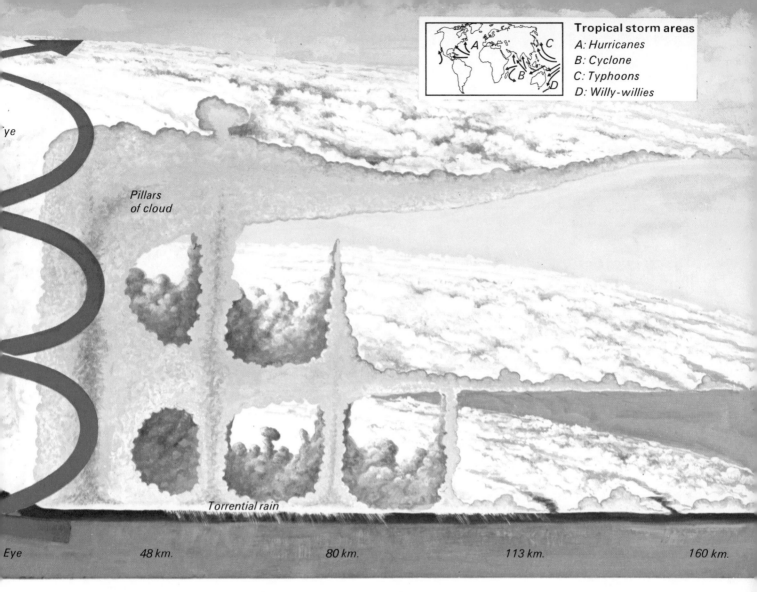

Eye

Pillars of cloud

Torrential rain

Eye	48 km.	80 km.	113 km.	160 km.

Pressure 947 mb.
Wind S.E.
Force 12

Pressure 981 mb.
Wind S.E.
Force 12

Pressure 982 mb.
Wind S.
Force 9

Pressure rising rapidly
Wind S.W.
Force 6

How the hurricanes get their names

During the hurricane season, weather stations keep a careful watch for the dreadful storms. In the U.S. a special department works all the time tracking them down with the help of aircraft, radar and satellite pictures.

When a hurricane is spotted, it is given a girl's name to identify it. The first storm of the season has a name beginning with "A", such as Audrey, the second a name beginning with "B", and so on. Their paths are then tracked and they are watched constantly.

▶ A Japanese print called *The Wave*. These vast waves, whipped up by the howling winds of a tropical storm, cause a great deal of damage.

29

Silent killers fog, ice and snow

Paralyzed by the forces of nature

In this age of technology, people have many high-speed methods of transport to carry them where they wish to go. Yet all these methods can fail as a result of sudden bad weather. The three types of weather which produce this chaos most frequently are fog, ice and snow.

The creeping peril of fog

Within a few hours it can paralyze a nation, and yet fog is still very difficult to forecast. The conditions have to be exactly right for it to form. The air must be full of water vapour. The temperature must be low enough to cool the earth's surface. The wind must be gentle enough to stir the foggy layers upward, but not strong enough to blow them away.

These conditions may only occur in scattered places, which is why a road may be partly clear and partly covered by dense fog.

The beautiful killers

Snow and ice, though beautiful to the winter holiday-maker, can also be killers. A sudden noise in the mountains may send millions of tons of snow sliding down onto houses and villages, burying them in a disastrous avalanche.

Warm rain falls on freezing cold metal and turns to layers of ice. The weight of this may cause ships to founder and force aircraft to land.

Warm rain which falls and freezes can also cause glazed frost. In a few minutes, telephone lines become thick with ice and break under the strain. Roads become death traps as they are covered by "black ice"

▼ Micro-photographs of snow flakes. Snow flakes can form many different patterns, but the shapes will always be six-sided.

▲ A familiar sight on roads in the winter. A sudden fall of snow has blocked the road and motorists have been forced to abandon cars and lorries.

A fog "sweep"

◄ A fog "sweep" being taken down. This inflatable chimney can be driven about on the back of a truck and is used to blow fog away. It is one of many new methods being used in an attempt to lessen fog danger.

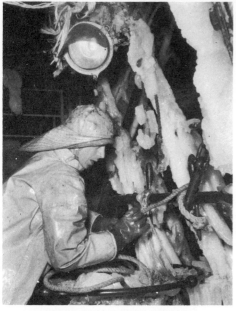

▲ Trawling for fish in winter is very unpleasant. This trawler is covered with sheets of heavy ice which must be removed by hand.

▶ These pictures show Stoke-on-Trent in England in 1900 and 1969, before and after the Clean Air Acts were passed. Smog (fog mixed with smoke and dirt) can get too thick for the sun to show through, and is very bad for health. People all over the world are becoming worried about air pollution.

1900

1969

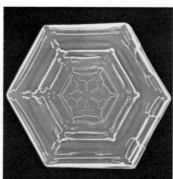

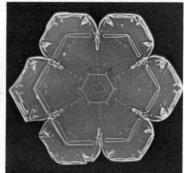

Climates large and small

◄ The climate describes the normal weather for an area. Sometimes this pattern is upset and there is very unusual weather. These trainee priests in Rome are enjoying an unusual fall of snow.

Usual weather

In some places, people know what the weather is likely to do. In India, where the monsoon operates, there are three definite seasons. Between December and February it is cold; from February until May it is hot, and between June and December it rains. This happens every year so it is the expected weather, or climate, of the country. Climate is long-term weather.

Weather in a nutshell

A country's climate may depend upon its whereabouts in the world, whether it is near the sea or not, and if it is mountainous or flat. But small areas can have their own "local" climates.

Houses in a narrow valley may be in a frost hollow. Cold, heavy air rolls down the hills and fills the valley with freezing air, giving it a colder climate than the surrounding area.

There are even micro-climates, tiny areas which each experience different weather. The climate of a shady wood will be very different from that of an open field with no shelter.

An important modern science

Climatology, or the study of climates, is an important science in many walks of life. It is most important for people such as farmers and gardeners who must know which areas of their land will best suit which crops or plants.

Architects also study climates. When planning new towns, with tall modern blocks separated by broad, open streets, they may be creating new and unexpected local climates.

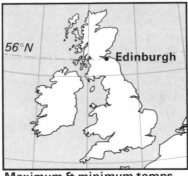

Maximum & minimum temps.

Jan. F M A M J J A S O N Dec.

0°C.

◄ ▲ The distance from the sea makes a great difference to the climate of a country. Edinburgh is very close to the sea and has a maritime climate with no extremes of weather. As the graph shows, it is neither very hot in the summer nor very cold in the winter.

◄ ▼ Moscow is the same distance from the equator as Edinburgh but being far from the sea has a continental climate. In the summer it can be very hot, while in winter even the trees are protected from the cold.

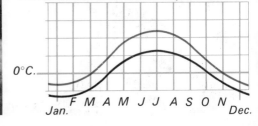

Maximum & minimum temperatures

0°C.

Jan. F M A M J J A S O N Dec.

Long grass and delicate flowers will grow in the moist, cool shade under trees in an orchard.

A greenhouse provides an artificial tropical climate throughout the year.

Peaches can be grown on a south-facing wall. They will be sheltered from the wind and receive hours of sunshine.

Cracks between paving stones and rockeries will provide a baking climate for sun-loving plants.

Plants in pots provide a cool, moist climate for shade-loving creatures.

Changes in climate through the ages

▲ In the Permian Era, 250 million years ago, many parts of the world which today have a temperate climate were barren deserts.

▲ During the Pleistocene Era, 300 thousand years ago, the same places were in the middle of an ice age.

▲ A garden consists of a mass of micro-climates. Every gardener knows that certain plants thrive in certain places. The micro-climate for each plant must be exactly right, and one that suits a shade-loving lily will not suit a sun-loving rock plant.

A gardener shows his skill by reproducing in some artificial way the climate that each plant would find in its natural home.

◄ The climates of the world seem to us to be always the same. In fact, they are constantly changing. Regions which have a mild climate today may have been both baking desert and freezing ice plateau since the world began. Some scientists think we are now entering a new ice age.

33

Has the weather changed history?

Sacred bones change the weather

For hundreds of years, the only way to travel long distances at sea was by using the wind. One country could only invade another country by this means if the weather was favourable.

In the 11th century, Duke William of Normandy wished to invade England. The weather was against him day after day and his army began to give up and go home. It is said that he carried sacred bones in procession along the cliffs and that the next day the weather changed.

Weather has also played a part in exploration. Many places have been discovered by accident, but many may have been missed because of the weather. In 1579, Sir Francis Drake sailed right past the great natural harbour of San Francisco because of fog.

A storm improves forecasting

In 1854, during the Crimean War, some French ships containing vital supplies were sunk in a terrible storm. This storm had passed right across Europe. If its path had been studied the French fleet could have been warned in advance and the supplies saved.

This disaster led to the first attempts to forecast future weather by studying present weather. It is always in times of war that the study of weather has become more efficient.

▲ When the Spanish Armada attacked England, the wind controlled the whole battle. It stopped the British admiral from leading his fleet to sea, but later it blew the remains of the Spanish fleet to disaster on the rocks.

▶ General Washington knew how to use the weather. In 1777, during the American War of Independence he and his army became trapped in deep mud. One night the mud froze, so he quickly moved out and caught the British by surprise.

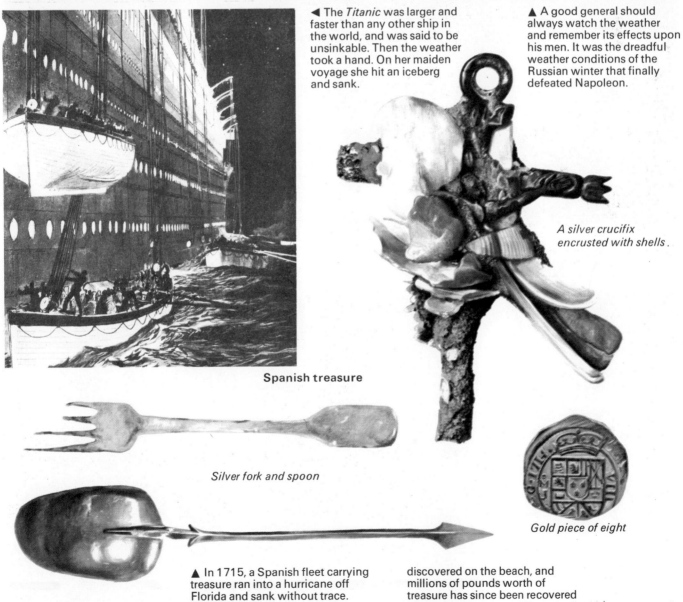

◄ The *Titanic* was larger and faster than any other ship in the world, and was said to be unsinkable. Then the weather took a hand. On her maiden voyage she hit an iceberg and sank.

▲ A good general should always watch the weather and remember its effects upon his men. It was the dreadful weather conditions of the Russian winter that finally defeated Napoleon.

A silver crucifix encrusted with shells.

Spanish treasure

Silver fork and spoon

Gold piece of eight

▲ In 1715, a Spanish fleet carrying treasure ran into a hurricane off Florida and sank without trace. Recently, gold pieces of eight were discovered on the beach, and millions of pounds worth of treasure has since been recovered from the sea.

Forecasting at home

Odd ways of knowing the weather

Before the weather was seriously studied, people had many odd ways of forecasting it. Country people noticed that animals seemed to know when the weather was about to change, so they watched them carefully.

Many theories grew up, and some of the old sayings have survived. They may sound strange nowadays, but there is often some scientific truth in them. The illustrations at the bottom of the page show some of the most common of these sayings.

▲ This doll's cobalt chloride skirt turns pink when the air is damp and blue when it is dry.

◄ In 1641, Giovanni Baliani put a water barometer outside his house. If he could see the cork figure floating on top, the pressure was high and the weather would probably be good; if the figure sank below his window, he knew it would be bad.

Old weather sayings

Christmas on the balcony means Easter in the embers

(French saying)

It is sure to be a dry moon if you can hang your hat on its horns

(Welsh saying)

A weather house

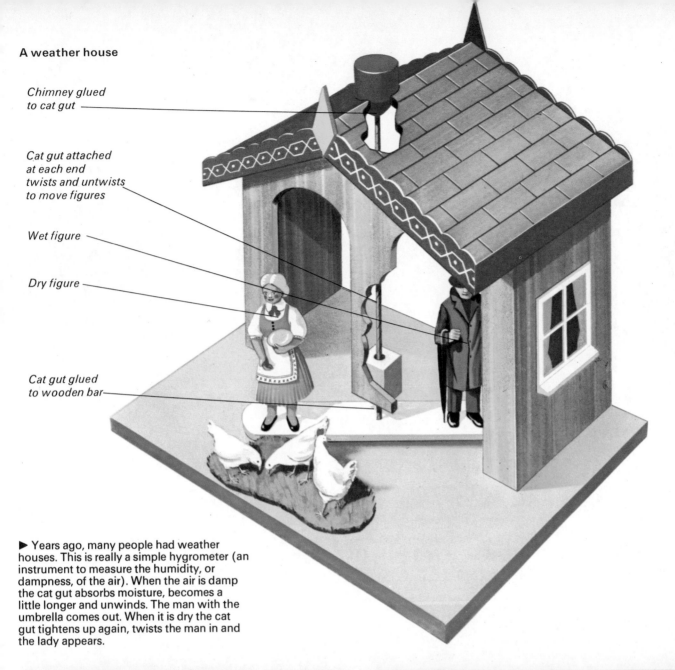

Chimney glued to cat gut

Cat gut attached at each end twists and untwists to move figures

Wet figure

Dry figure

Cat gut glued to wooden bar

▶ Years ago, many people had weather houses. This is really a simple hygrometer (an instrument to measure the humidity, or dampness, of the air). When the air is damp the cat gut absorbs moisture, becomes a little longer and unwinds. The man with the umbrella comes out. When it is dry the cat gut tightens up again, twists the man in and the lady appears.

**Red sky at night, shepherd's delight
Red sky in the morning, shepherd's warning**

(English saying)

One swallow does not make a summer

(German saying)

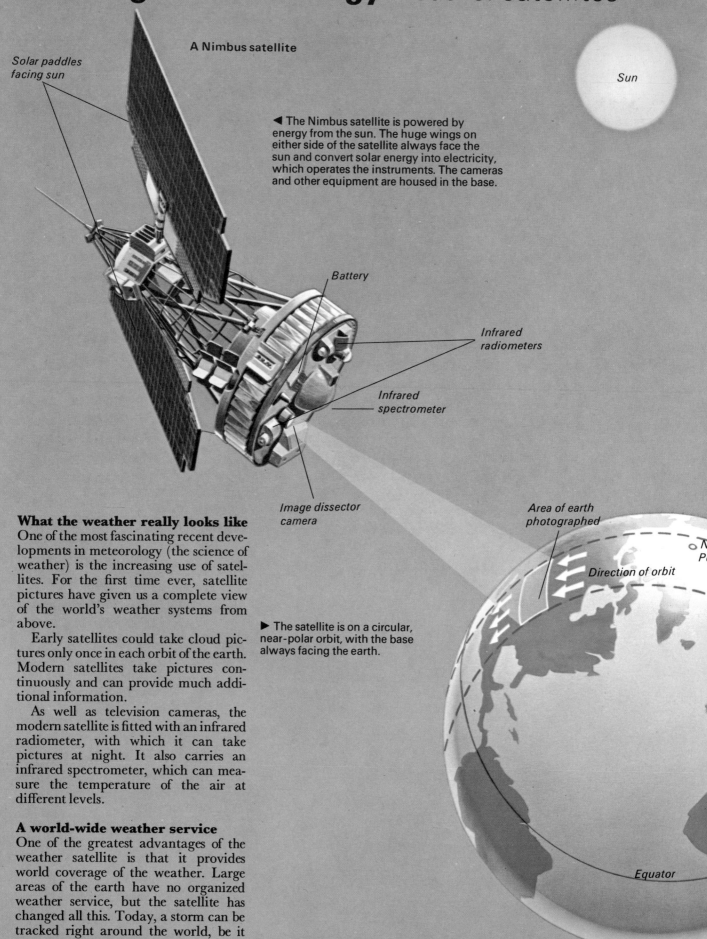

A Nimbus satellite

Solar paddles
facing sun

Sun

◄ The Nimbus satellite is powered by
energy from the sun. The huge wings on
either side of the satellite always face the
sun and convert solar energy into electricity,
which operates the instruments. The cameras
and other equipment are housed in the base.

Battery

Infrared
radiometers

Infrared
spectrometer

Image dissector
camera

Area of earth
photographed

N•
Po

Direction of orbit

► The satellite is on a circular,
near-polar orbit, with the base
always facing the earth.

Equator

What the weather really looks like

One of the most fascinating recent deve-
lopments in meteorology (the science of
weather) is the increasing use of satellites. For the first time ever, satellite
pictures have given us a complete view
of the world's weather systems from
above.

Early satellites could take cloud pictures only once in each orbit of the earth.
Modern satellites take pictures con-
tinuously and can provide much addi-
tional information.

As well as television cameras, the
modern satellite is fitted with an infrared
radiometer, with which it can take
pictures at night. It also carries an
infrared spectrometer, which can measure the temperature of the air at
different levels.

A world-wide weather service

One of the greatest advantages of the
weather satellite is that it provides
world coverage of the weather. Large
areas of the earth have no organized
weather service, but the satellite has
changed all this. Today, a storm can be
tracked right around the world, be it
over town, mountain or ocean.

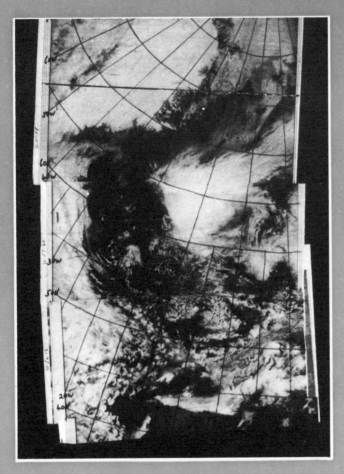

▲ This is a cloud mosaic, a picture made up from three separate photographs. It shows a whirling mass of cloud between Iceland and Norway with the British Isles just visible near the bottom.

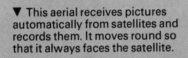

▼ This aerial receives pictures automatically from satellites and records them. It moves round so that it always faces the satellite.

▲ This was taken by the Nimbus III infra-red radiometer and not by a camera. It shows the British Isles, Europe and the Mediterranean Sea. A depression can be seen over Iceland.

The secret code of the weather men

How a synoptic chart is made

▼ All weather stations send frequent weather reports to a central office. First, the report is translated into one line of numbers, in groups of five figures.

▼ The weather centre receives the coded messages from many stations. The code is internationally used. Millions of reports pour out of teleprinters every day.

iiIII	Nddff	VVwwW	PPPTT	$N_h C_L h C_M C_H$	$T_d T_d$app	7RRjj	$8 N_s C h_s h_s$
03772	61815	40618	15211	52460	09020	70615	

ii	Block No. (for example British Isles)
III	Station No. (for example Heathrow Airport)
N	Fraction of sky covered by cloud (in eighths)
dd	Surface wind direction, in tens of degrees
ff	Surface wind speed, in knots
VV	Visibility, in nautical miles
ww	Present weather
W	Past weather
PPP	Mean sea-level air pressure, in millibars
TT	Dry-bulb temperature, in °C.
N_h	Amount of cloud
C_L	Type of low cloud
h	Height of base of low cloud
C_M	Type of medium cloud
C_H	Type of high cloud
$T_d T_d$	Dew-point temperature
a	How the barometer is changing, i.e. increasing or decreasing
pp	How much it is increasing or decreasing
7	Indicator figure of seventh group
RR	Rainfall, in millimetres
jj	Maximum temperature
8	Indicator figure of eighth group (optional group)
N_s	Amount of lowest cloud
$C h_s$	Type of lowest cloud
h_s	Height of lowest cloud

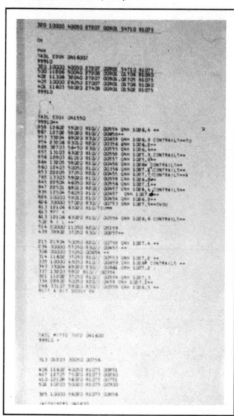

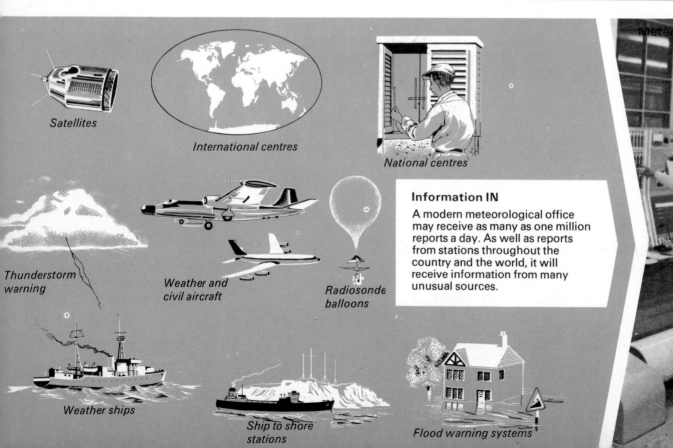

Satellites

International centres

National centres

Meteorological centre

Thunderstorm warning

Weather and civil aircraft

Radiosonde balloons

Information IN
A modern meteorological office may receive as many as one million reports a day. As well as reports from stations throughout the country and the world, it will receive information from many unusual sources.

Weather ships

Ship to shore stations

Flood warning systems

The station model

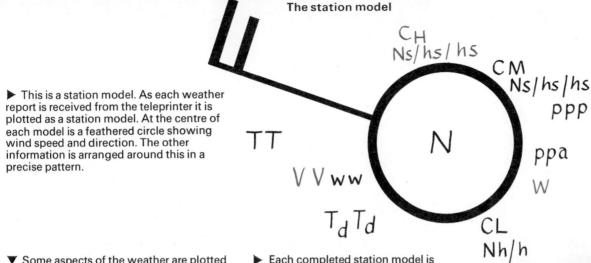

▶ This is a station model. As each weather report is received from the teleprinter it is plotted as a station model. At the centre of each model is a feathered circle showing wind speed and direction. The other information is arranged around this in a precise pattern.

Labels on the station model: CH Ns/hs/hs, CM Ns/hs/hs, ppp, ppa, w, CL Nh/h, N, TT, VV ww, $T_d T_d$

▼ Some aspects of the weather are plotted in their numbered code, but some are translated into symbols. The present weather (ww) information is translated into a symbol, and this chart shows how the symbols are worked out. There are 99 possible variations.

▶ Each completed station model is plotted in position on a map. When information from all the stations has been plotted the map is ready for analysis. The isobars and fronts are put in, and then the forecaster takes over.

WW	0	1	2	3	4	5	6	7	8	9
00						∞	S	$		
10										
20										
30										
40										
50										
60										
70										△
80										
90										

Symbol key:
- , Drizzle
- • Rain
- * Snow
- ▲ Hail
- : Sleet
- ▽ Showers
- ≡ Fog
- < Lightning
- Thunderstorm
- ∿ Freezing
- Dust or sand-storm

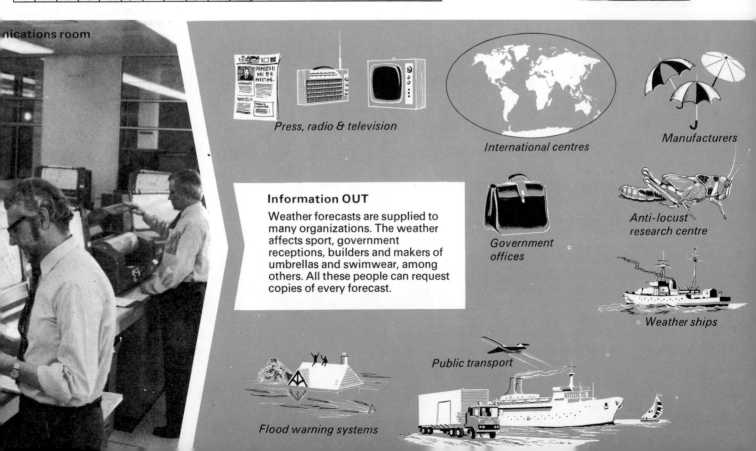

nications room

Press, radio & television

International centres

Manufacturers

Information OUT

Weather forecasts are supplied to many organizations. The weather affects sport, government receptions, builders and makers of umbrellas and swimwear, among others. All these people can request copies of every forecast.

Government offices

Anti-locust research centre

Weather ships

Public transport

Flood warning systems

The future

Automatic reporting stations

Meteorology is a science which alters almost from day to day. The great advances made by the satellite in the last 15 years have opened up new possibilities in weather forecasting.

There are still not enough reporting stations in areas where few people live, so the future will probably see an increase in automatic weather stations. They will be triggered by a weather satellite as it passes overhead and may be situated in very unlikely places. For some years now an experimental one has been strapped to the back of an unfortunate elk.

Improvements in forecasting

As more information is analyzed by computers, weather forecasting will improve. Already, forecasts are becoming accurate for four-day periods and monthly forecasts are issued.

There are now computers which can store up to 4,000 million pieces of information and miniature computers are being made. So it is not unreasonable to foresee the day when a satellite with built-in computer will process all its information and feed back a forecast for the area over which it is passing.

Boreholes to the centre of the earth

The future may also bring great advances in the control of the weather. People living in towns of the future may not even notice the weather. Shops and offices will be in great indoor centres with air-conditioning and heating, so it may never be necessary to go outside.

A vast amount of energy would be needed to control the weather. Cloud-seeding to produce rain is now quite common but is not always successful. It has been suggested that the power of the earth itself could be used to help control the weather.

Boreholes would be plunged far into the earth, producing great currents of hot air. These would create lines of clouds, which could then be seeded to produce rain where it is needed.

Schemes like these could alter our whole way of life, but until they are tried out it is the weather which will control us rather than we who will control the weather.

Weather satellites will trigger automatic receiving stations as they pass across the sky.

Boreholes may be sunk through the earth's crust to tap the energy of the earth. The hot air from these will create clouds.

Energy from fossil fuels may be in short supply. Heat from the sun may be used to convert water into steam to drive electric generators.

An automatic weather station. It can be placed in areas remote from civilization to report the weather to the satellite above.

Street corners will be equipped with air pollution units. Fumes will be sucked in at the base, the air cleaned and puffed out from the top.

An aircraft seeds a cloud with dry ice or silver iodide to encourage rain to fall.

Temperature, amount of light and humidity will all be controlled so that any type of plant can be grown. Windows will be double glazed to avoid condensation and heat loss.

Each television set will be equipped with controls that can fade the programme and replace it with the weather map whenever required.

The weather satellite will transmit a steady stream of signals. An aerial on every house will be capable of receiving them.

ps and plants will grow der glass in artificial ates.

ght and fresh air will nufactured and windows o longer be required.

VIDEO·101

S→N

Projects build your own weather station

Perhaps you would like to study the weather? For accurate scientific work you would need standardized instruments, but it is interesting to compare one day with another. This can be done with simple homemade equipment. In fact, early meteorologists only had instruments like the ones on this page.

There are many things you can do without any instruments at all. You can keep a scrapbook in which you collect photos of different clouds and newspaper cuttings reporting any stories dealing with the weather. Once you start looking you may be surprised.

You might also like to keep a weather diary. Try to find out if there is any relationship between the direction of the wind and the weather.

Another interesting idea is to collect weather rhymes like the ones in this book. See if you can find out why so many appear to work. There may be some scientific principle behind them.

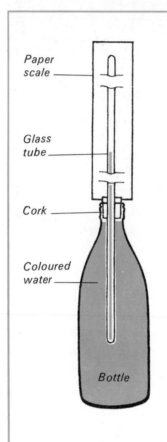

Paper scale

Glass tube

Cork

Coloured water

Bottle

Water thermometer

The first instrument you will need is a thermometer. If you cannot buy one it is fairly easy to make one. You will need a narrow-necked bottle with a cork to fit, a piece of narrow bore glass tubing and some coloured water.

Pass the glass tubing through the cork, taking great care not to cut yourself, then fill the bottle with the water and push the cork in hard. You will see that the water is forced a little way up the tube. Now it is all ready for use, and you may be surprised how sensitive it is. If you glue a piece of card to the tube you will be able to mark off different temperatures.

To compare this with a real thermometer you must place them both in a saucepan of water. When the coloured water has stopped falling in the tube you can mark off this level and label it with the temperature from the other thermometer.

Carefully warm the water until the bought thermometer is reading ten degrees higher. Mark this new level on your tube. If you divide the space between these two readings into ten equal parts these marks will measure degrees. Similar marks up and down will calibrate your instrument.

An anemometer

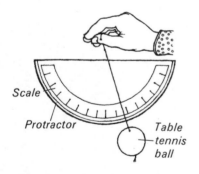

Scale

Protractor

Table tennis ball

To make an easy anemometer you need a 180° protractor, a table tennis ball and a length of thread. Glue one end of the thread to the ball and the other to the centre of the protractor. Hold the instrument in the wind so that the wind is blowing along the protractor. The light ball will be blown backwards and the thread will move along the protractor. By using the Beaufort wind scale (Page 14) you can make a scale and attach it to the protractor.

Rain gauge

A rain gauge is a straightforward instrument. It is also one of the oldest, for it was used in the 15th century.

You will need a straight-sided tin, a funnel which fits it as closely as possible and a glass jar. First, you must calibrate your glass measure. Fill the tin with water to a depth of 20 mm. Pour the water into the glass jar and mark the level with a line. The distance from the line to the bottom can be divided into 20 equal parts and it will measure millimetres.

Now take the tin and stick a band of foam rubber around the inside to hold the funnel in place. Remember that there must not be a gap between the tin and the funnel. Place the jam jar in the tin and the funnel in the jar, with the top resting on the foam rubber. You can now use the rain gauge.

In weather stations they are very careful to cut the grass to a special length and make sure that the top of the funnel is above grass level, so that no water can splash in and alter the level.

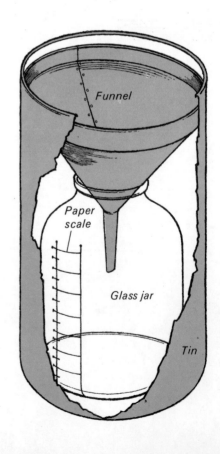

Funnel

Paper scale

Glass jar

Tin

Barometers to measure air pressure

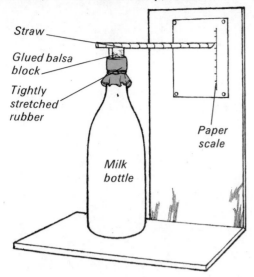

Straw

Glued balsa block

Tightly stretched rubber

Milk bottle

Paper scale

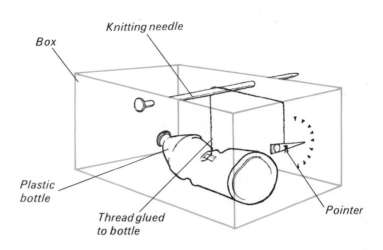

Box

Knitting needle

Plastic bottle

Thread glued to bottle

Pointer

Another instrument you will need is a simple barometer. For this you will need a milk bottle. Stretch a taut cover of balloon rubber across the top. To the centre of this stick a drinking straw. This straw will act as a pointer and if you attach a simple scale behind it you will be able to see if the pressure is high or low. As the air pressure pushes down on the rubber the pointer will move upwards. The higher the pressure the more the pointer will move.

It is also possible to make an aneroid barometer. For this you will need a plastic squeezy bottle. First push out some of the air by squeezing and then seal up the bottle with plastic cement. Stick the bottle on its side to a base board inside a box. To the top surface of the bottle attach a piece of terylene thread. Pass this thread round a knitting needle and over the edge of the box. Attach the end to a pointer on the side of the box and mark a scale next to it.

If you do not wish to make a barometer you can measure air pressure with the help of an altimeter. You can buy an old aircraft altimeter from a government surplus store which will make an excellent barometer. Remember that if you wish to read the air pressure you must turn the knob at the bottom until the hands read 0. You can then read the pressure in the window at the bottom.

A Stevenson screen made of tins

In the early days of weather recording people did not realize the importance of the place in which they kept their thermometers. It makes a great difference to the reading. One man recorded temperatures for years with the thermometer hanging his living room.

There are also many things outside which will influence your readings. Try taking them in the sun, and then in the shade or around a draughty corner. All these factors must be removed, so you must construct a container or screen to hold the instruments.

The screen used in weather stations is called a Stevenson screen but is rather difficult to make. You can make a good screen out of two tins, one larger than the other. Mount one inside the other to allow a free flow of air. Fix them to a base board with a wooden block to support your thermometer and you will have a very efficient screen.

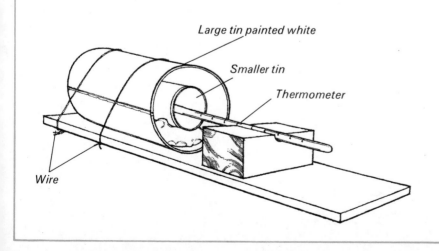

Large tin painted white

Smaller tin

Thermometer

Wire

A wind vane

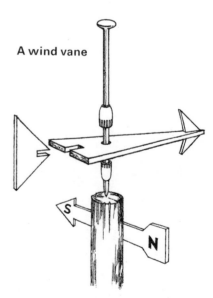

S

N

One of the simplest instruments to make is a wind vane. Many aerodromes use a sock hanging in the wind. This is a good guide because it also shows very roughly how strong the wind is, but the traditional vane is similar to the weather cock you see on church towers.

You can make any flat shape on a bar and use it as a wind vane, but remember that the two sides must balance on the supporting spindle. Take care where you position the wind vane as eddies can whip round the corners of buildings which will give an entirely wrong direction.

45

Studying the weather

Wet and dry bulb hygrometer

To measure the humidity you will need a hygrometer. For this you need two similar thermometers placed side by side against a board. One of them must have a wick wrapped around the bulb. For this a hollow football lace is useful.

Dip the lace into a small container of water. The water in the container will travel up the wick to evaporate round the bulb. This will cool it so that it will read a lower temperature than the other thermometer. When the air is wet, very little water will evaporate, and the difference between the two readings will be small. If the air is very dry, much water will evaporate and cool the bulb and the difference will be very great.

To use the hygrometer, first read the temperature as recorded on the normal or dry bulb thermometer. This is the normal outside temperature. Now read the temperature recorded on the wet bulb thermometer. This will be a few degrees lower. Now look at the table below. Choose the column that corresponds with the dry bulb temperature. Follow this column down until you reach the number of degrees that the wet bulb temperature is below the dry bulb temperature. Where these two lines meet is the relative humidity.

For example, if the dry bulb temperature is 17·5° C, and the difference is 3°, you will see from the table that the relative humidity is 74%.

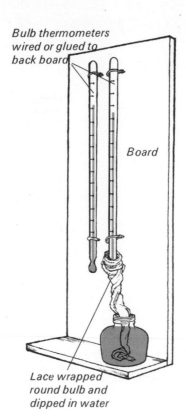

Bulb thermometers wired or glued to back board

Board

Lace wrapped round bulb and dipped in water

Difference between wet and dry bulb in degrees	Dry bulb temperatures				
	15-16°	16-17°	17-18°	18-19°	19-20°
1	88%	90%	91%	92%	92%
1.5	83%	85%	86%	87%	88%
2	77%	81%	82%	83%	84%
2.5	74%	77%	78%	79%	80%
3	67%	72%	74%	75%	77%
3.5	64%	68%	70%	71%	73%
4	60%	63%	66%	68%	70%
4.5	55%	60%	62%	64%	66%
5	50%	55%	58%	61%	63%
5.5	47%	52%	55%	57%	60%
6	45%	47%	51%	53%	57%
6.5	40%	44%	47%	50%	53%
7	37%	41%	44%	48%	50%
7.5	34%	37%	40%	44%	48%

Glossary

anemometer an instrument for measuring the speed of the wind.

anticyclone a region of high air pressure. The air flows outwards with a spiral movement.

barometer an instrument for measuring air pressure, either using mercury or a vacuum chamber.

condensation the process by which liquid water is formed from invisible water vapour, as in cloud formation.

Coriolis effect the effect of the spin of the earth upon moving objects. In the Northern Hemisphere moving air is deflected to the right; in the Southern Hemisphere, it is deflected to the left.

cyclone a cyclone or "depression" is a region of low air pressure. Air flows spirally inwards forming a vortex (like water running down the plughole of a bath).

Hadley cell the circular movement of air around the world caused by unequal heating.

inversion a layer in the atmosphere in which temperature increases with height instead of decreasing, causing rising air to be trapped beneath.

isobars lines drawn on a chart to connect places with equal air pressure.

millibar the unit in which atmospheric pressure is measured; equal to 1,000 dynes per square cm.
1 millibar = 0.7504 mm. = 0.02853 in. of a mercury column.

ozone a molecule of oxygen formed by three oxygen atoms instead of two. Part of the chemical make-up of the atmosphere.

polar front a semi-permanent zone separating the heavy cold polar air from other air masses.

stable air sinking air that tends to cause fog and bad visibility.

synoptic chart a map showing station models, fronts and isobars, which is analyzed to produce a weather forecast.

thermals rising currents of heated air.

unstable air air which tends to rise, giving showers and thunderstorms.

Index

Illustration Credits

Key to the positions of illustrations: (T) top, (C) centre,
(B) bottom, and combinations; for example (TR) top right,
or (CL) centre left

Artists
Ron Hayward Ass. 40-1
David Jefferies 42-3
Eric Jewell Ass. 11, 12-3, 22-3, 27, 37 (T), 38
John Mousedale/Freelance Presentations 44-7
Janet Munch/Freelance Presentations 14-5, 33
Tony Payne 18-9, 24-5
Colin Rose 7, 14 (T), 16-7, 21, 22(T), 32
John Shackell 10-1, 36, 37 (B)
John Smith 3, 4-5, 8-9, 28-9, 35

Photographs and Prints
Associated Press 7 (BL), 16
Australian News and Information Bureau 3 (BL), 7 (TR)
Automobile Association 30 (T)
Corporal Bender 18 (R)
T. Bradbury 23 (T)
British Ceramic Research Association 31 (R)
British Museum 28 (R)
Central Electricity Generating Board 6 (BL)
N. Elkins 18 (C)

F.A.O. 20 (BR)
J. Hollington 23 (B)
J. Allen Cash 17 (R)
John M. Davis & Ass. 31 (L)
Keystone Press Agency 26 (TR)
Mansell Collection 26 (TL)
Mary Evans Picture Library 12 (T), 26 (BL), 34 (B)
Meteorological Office, Bracknell/Crown Copyright 6 (T)
  27, 39, 40, 41
Jean Mohr 20 (BL)
National Centre for Atmospheric Research, Boulder,
  Colorado 12 (B)
National Maritime Museum 15
Philippines Embassy 18 (L)
Picturepoint 17 (L)
Radio Times Hulton Picture Library 34 (T), 35 (T), 35 (E
Rex Features 32 (T)
N. Scott 5 (B)
Shell 6 (BR)
Society for Cultural Relations with the U.S.S.R. 32 (B)
South African Tourist Corp. 21 (B)
Syndication International 32 (C)
Transworld Feature Syndicate 7 (TL)
United Press International 7 (BR)
Zeiss 30-1 (B)